P9-DOB-892

BENNETT'S FABLES

Christmas 1978
from
Mom & Dad

— the pictures for the children
& the reading for the adults —

BENNETT'S FABLES

FROM AESOP AND OTHERS

TRANSLATED INTO HUMAN NATURE BY CHARLES H. BENNETT

FOREWORD BY GERALD GOTTLIEB

A STUDIO BOOK · THE VIKING PRESS · NEW YORK

Introduction Copyright in all Countries of the International
Copyright Union by Viking Penguin Inc., 1978
All rights reserved
Published in 1978 by The Viking Press
625 Madison Avenue, New York, N.Y. 10022
Published simultaneously in Canada by
Penguin Books Canada Limited

Library of Congress Cataloging in Publication Data
Bennett, Charles Henry, 1829–1867.
Bennett's fables from Aesop and others.
(A Studio book)
Reprint of the 1857 ed. published by W. Kent, London, under title: The
fables of Aesop and others, translated into human nature.
1. Fables. I. Title. II. Title: Fables from Aesop and others.
PN982.B4   1978   398.2'45   78-4858

ISBN 0–670–15807–0

Set in Caslon Lino and Goudy Handtooled
Printed in Japan

CONTENTS

FOREWORD

The earliest human beings lived surrounded by animals. From out of this intertwining of the lives of man and beast there grew folklore, in the form of tales peopled by animals who behaved like humans. And after a time a clever person, a canny sophisticate who may have been named Aesop, shaped some of the folktales into fables.

The most striking characteristic of a fable, of course, is that it points a moral. It sets foxes, mice, lions, even trees and flowers and inanimate objects, to acting and conversing as if they were people; and in the process it demonstrates something about the nature of human life. A fable concerning a dog strutting in a manger reminds us that power corrupts. A fable about a fox who decides that some grapes he cannot manage to reach must certainly be sour recalls our human need to mask our failures. Aesop, who probably lived on the Greek island of Samos in the sixth century B.C., is supposed to have concocted his fables for the use of orators who wanted pithy anecdotes to enliven their discourses. A speaker in ancient Athens trying to drive home a point about the greed or vanity of a particular politician must have been delighted to have at hand one of Aesop's ingeniously effective fables—"The Dog and the Shadow," perhaps, or "The Frog and the Ox."

People have been no less delighted ever since. People, that is, both old and young; the allure of Aesop has seldom known any boundaries of age. The fables were not originally intended for children, but children have seized them hungrily from the first. The phrase "for all ages" has never been so aptly applied as to Aesop. And "timeless" is another description that is apt; after all the centuries, the fables are still graphic, pertinent, and marvelously enjoyable. The joy they afford is of a special kind. It contains such things as our satisfaction at seeing the braggart deflated and the trickster outwitted, and our pleasure at having our own minor virtues (thrift, perhaps, or prudence) applauded. These satisfactions and pleasures may be small, but they are real, and they are comforting. The scale is indeed rather small: the fables do not often take up great moral questions. Instead, they present a pragmatic folk-shrewdness. They offer little nuggets of succinct, homey wisdom centering on commonplace happenings and the everyday, kitchen-and-barnyard truths of human nature.

Whether or not Aesop ever really existed, he certainly did not produce all the many fables that are now gathered under his name. Some of them come from sources as far from the island of Samos as the subcontinent of India. But most of the fables show the same kind of mind at work. It is a mind that is at once shrewd, detached, amused, cynical, and witty. It is a mind that seems to have reappeared in the middle of the nineteenth century in the person of an Englishman named Charles Henry Bennett.

He was born in 1829, and he was not the first such reincarnation of Aesop. There had been an earlier one in seventeenth-century France, in the shape of Jean de la Fontaine. In every generation, in fact, certain gifted writers have adapted and reinterpreted the fables and put them to good use. Charles H. Bennett's gifts, however, were greater than most. He was not blessed merely with the perceptiveness and the wry wisdom of an Aesop; he also happened to be a remarkable comic artist.

The fables have of course attracted artists from the very beginning. An Aesop was among the first books to appear in print after movable type was perfected in the mid-fifteenth century, and a collection of the fables was one of the first printed books to receive the benefit of illustrations. But few illustrators of Aesop have worked with texts that they themselves wrote. Charles Bennett not only produced his own versions of the fables; he also produced a book that in time would become one of the most admired and influential of all the illustrated books to appear in England in the nineteenth century—a century that witnessed the greatest flowering of book illustration in modern English history.

The Fables of Aesop and Others Translated into Human Nature (to give the book its full original title) was published in 1857, when Queen Victoria had been on the throne for twenty years. It is a thoroughly Victorian production, informed by the values and preoccupations of the age. Bennett shared all these; but he was also an unusually perceptive and mordacious man, a man of some genius. He used this genius to satirize adroitly, sometimes wickedly, the types he saw about him. And in performing his satire he often seemed to be balancing on a tight-rope stretched between the human world and the world of animals.

In this he owed a debt to some predecessors. The image of a being simultaneously human and animal—a man with the head of a bird, for example—goes back at least three or four thousand years, to wall paintings in Egyptian tombs. It is far older than Aesop. Whether done for mystic, moral, or comic effect, such images have always held a fascination for us. In France in the 1830s the caricaturist and artist-lithographer J.-I.-I. Gérard, known as Grandville, employed the concept strikingly in —to name but one instance among many—his illustrations to La Fontaine. The influence of Grandville on John Tenniel's drawings for *Alice in Wonderland* has been remarked upon before now; but *Alice* did not appear until 1865, and Charles Bennett's *Fables of Aesop and Others* was published in 1857. Grandville's lion-headed or frog-headed men, and his pompous, grave insects, erect on their hind legs and deep in conversation with one another, are the pictorial ancestors of Bennett's lobsters in uniform, of his frock-coated moles and lambs, of his wolves wearing rakish caps. Like Grandville, Bennett reveled in visual witticisms about the similarities between animals and humans. In his work as a staff member of the great satiric magazine *Punch,* where Bennett spent the final two years of his short life, this preoccupation resulted in some memorable caricatures of Victorian politicians: Disraeli as a hedgehog, Gladstone as a small dog, Lord John Russell as a coroneted rooster. Bennett's colleagues on *Punch* appreciated his uncommon talent, and they were stunned by his early death (he was but thirty-seven). Their obituary of him described his imagination as "graceful and curious," and spoke of the "facile execution and singular subtlety of fancy" that characterized his work. To raise money for Bennett's widow and children, his colleagues staged an amateur theatrical performance (one of the skits was entitled "A Sheep in Wolf's Clothing"). The evening was a great success, for he was a well-loved man.

Reading the introductory note Charles Henry Bennett wrote to *The*

Fables of Aesop and Others Translated into Human Nature, one might easily gather that the man behind the book was a stereotypical Victorian gentleman, straightforward and bluff. But there is a vignette on the book's title page which carries a more sardonic suggestion. The vignette shows a man gazing into a mirror at his reflection, and his reflection is a fox.

GERALD GOTTLIEB
Curator of Early Children's Books
The Pierpont Morgan Library

Charles H. Bennett drew the designs for his illustrations directly on the wood blocks that were to be used to print the pictures. The blocks were then engraved, following Bennett's designs, by Joseph Swain, the chief engraver for *Punch*. The printing was done in black-and-white, after which the illustrations for those copies designated to be sold as "10s. 6d. Coloured" were colored by hand.

The copy of *The Fables of Aesop and Others Translated into Human Nature* which the present edition reproduces is a hand-colored copy from the first edition. It is the property of The Pierpont Morgan Library in New York City. It came to the Morgan Library in 1976, as part of a bequest of rare and valuable books and manuscripts from the library of Miss Tessie Jones, daughter of the celebrated American book collector Herschel V. Jones.

INTRODUCTION

The Author of this little Book knows that he has much to learn, and even believes that he has something to forget. He has had one success ("Shadows"), but knowing how many shortcomings must have been forgiven before so unanimously favorable a verdict could have been arrived at, he is encouraged to put forward this book of "Fables Translated into Human Nature," as little more than a promise of what (God willing) he hopes to attempt.

It may be as well to state that this is but the first half of the originally projected work, and that contingent on the success of this instalment the remainder will be published next year.*

The Design which forms the Frontispiece to this Book, and which is therefore presumed to be somewhat typical of the intention of Fable, represents Man tried at the Court of the Lion for the ill-treatment of a Horse. It will be seen that Man has the worst of it; while his Victim has secured the Shark for his Solicitor, and the Fox, Ape, and Vulture for Counsel; the woe-begone Defendant has had to make shift with Wolf, Dog, Ass, and Daw. The Rat and the Rabbit, the Elephant and the Sheep, even the Turkey and the little Birds, seem to have given it against him, irrespective of the "Silence" of the Parrot Usher. The Clerk of the Arraigns looks through his spectacles, and the Bull has gone to sleep in a corner.

CHARLES H. BENNETT

London,
  October, 1857

---

* Apparently "the success of this instalment" was insufficient, for no sequel was ever published.—G.G.

The Wolf and the Lamb

As a hungry thief of a Wolf was loitering at the end of a lonely road, there passed by a mild-faced, timid-looking Lamb, who was returning to the maternal pen. As the Lamb wore a fine fleecy coat and carried about him many signs of good living, the marauder's jaws watered at the prospect of a supper.

"What do you mean," said he, glaring upon the little traveller with his fierce eyes, "by taking up so much of the path where I am walking?"

The Lamb, frightened at the Wolf's angry tone and terrible aspect, told him that, with all due submission, he could not conceive how his walking on such a wide path could occasion him any inconvenience.

"What!" exclaimed the Wolf, seemingly in great anger and indignation; "you are as impudent as your father, the magistrate's dog, with the letters on his collar, who seized me by the throat last year, and caused me to be kept in a cage for three months—having all my beautiful hair cut off!"

"If you will believe me," said the innocent Lamb, "my parents are poor simple creatures who live entirely by green stuffs, in Lambeth Walk, hard by; we are none of us hunters of your species."

"Ah! I see it's no use talking to you," said the Wolf, drawing up close to him, "it runs in the blood of your family to hate us Wolves; and therefore, as we have come so conveniently together, I'll just pay off a few of your forefathers' scores before we part."

So saying, he leapt at the throat of the poor Pet Lamb from behind, and garotted him with his own pretty gold-studded collar.

MORAL

If you have made up your mind to hang your dog, any rope will do for the purpose.

Dear Keith & Don,

I ordered this book from the Metropolitan Museum of Art. It is a 2nd printing, the 1st printing was sold out. I thought it was going to be geared for children, but it isn't. It is a riot with its long involved Victorian style sentences and most peculiar "moral"

INTRODUCTION

The Author of this little Book knows that he has much to learn, and even believes that he has something to forget. He has had one success ("Shadows"), but knowing how many shortcomings must have been forgiven before so unanimously favorable a verdict could have been arrived at, he is encouraged to put forward this book of "Fables Translated into Human Nature," as little more than a promise of what (God willing) he hopes to attempt.

It may be as well to state that this is but the first half of the originally projected work, and that contingent on the success of this instalment the remainder will be published next year.*

The Design which forms the Frontispiece to this Book, and which is therefore presumed to be somewhat typical of the intention of Fable, represents Man tried at the Court of the Lion for the ill-treatment of a Horse. It will be seen that Man has the worst of it; while his Victim has secured the Shark for his Solicitor, and the Fox, Ape, and Vulture for Counsel; the woe-begone Defendant has had to make shift with Wolf, Dog, Ass, and Daw. The Rat and the Rabbit, the Elephant and the Sheep, even the Turkey and the little Birds, seem to have given it against him, irrespective of the "Silence" of the Parrot Usher. The Clerk of the Arraigns looks through his spectacles, and the Bull has gone to sleep in a corner.

CHARLES H. BENNETT

London,
    October, 1857

* Apparently "the success of this instalment" was insufficient, for no sequel was ever published.—G.G.

The Wolf and the Lamb

As a hungry thief of a Wolf was loitering at the end of a lonely road, there passed by a mild-faced, timid-looking Lamb, who was returning to the maternal pen. As the Lamb wore a fine fleecy coat and carried about him many signs of good living, the marauder's jaws watered at the prospect of a supper.

"What do you mean," said he, glaring upon the little traveller with his fierce eyes, "by taking up so much of the path where I am walking?"

The Lamb, frightened at the Wolf's angry tone and terrible aspect, told him that, with all due submission, he could not conceive how his walking on such a wide path could occasion him any inconvenience.

"What!" exclaimed the Wolf, seemingly in great anger and indignation; "you are as impudent as your father, the magistrate's dog, with the letters on his collar, who seized me by the throat last year, and caused me to be kept in a cage for three months—having all my beautiful hair cut off!"

"If you will believe me," said the innocent Lamb, "my parents are poor simple creatures who live entirely by green stuffs, in Lambeth Walk, hard by; we are none of us hunters of your species."

"Ah! I see it's no use talking to you," said the Wolf, drawing up close to him, "it runs in the blood of your family to hate us Wolves; and therefore, as we have come so conveniently together, I'll just pay off a few of your forefathers' scores before we part."

So saying, he leapt at the throat of the poor Pet Lamb from behind, and garotted him with his own pretty gold-studded collar.

MORAL

If you have made up your mind to hang your dog, any rope will do for the purpose.

Charles. H. Bennett.

The Frog and the Ox

As a splendid Ox—who, by right of the great family he belonged to, was permitted to disport himself as he pleased in the fashionable parks of London—was taking his afternoon stroll, an envious, tawdry-coated little Frog, that stood gaping at him hard-by, called out to certain of his fellows (who had hopped thither in his company all the way from the Fleet Ditch in the City) to take particular notice of the enormous size of the first-mentioned animal.

"And see," he said, "if I don't make the biggest swell of the two."

So he puffed himself up, once, twice, and again, and went still swelling on in impotent emulation, till in the end—spite of the cautions of his brother frogs—he burst himself.

MORAL

The humble citizen who strives, by mere inflation, to make as great an outward appearance as his substantial neighbour, must inevitably go to pieces.

SWAIN SC

Charles H. Bennett

The Ass in a Lion's Skin

There was a dreadful young Ass once, who prevailed upon the old Asses, his indulgent parents, to obtain for him a Lion's skin, in which to masquerade about the world. At great cost and inconvenience to themselves, they provided him with the disguise he had begged for; and, clothed in it, he strutted forth believing himself a very Lion, and causing men to flee before him in terror.

But it chanced in the end that, partly by the length of his ears, and partly by the discordance of his bray when he tried roaring, he was discovered, and the Lions with whom he had sought to herd fell upon him so mercilessly, that he only saved himself by flight, leaving his brave coat behind him, while men on every side laughed at and pelted him as he flew to his native common.

MORAL
It is not the cocked hat that makes the Warrior.

Swain

C. H. Bennett

The Lobster and His Mother

A greenish young Lobster crawling along the Strand with his mother (who, being old and learned, had attained to a deep Blue complexion) was struck by the appearance of a specimen of his own tribe—evidently laid out for show—whose shell-jacket was of a brilliant red. Young, ignorant, and vain, he viewed the dazzling spectacle with admiration and envy.

"Behold," he said, addressing his parent, "the beauty and splendour of one of our family, thus decked out in glorious scarlet. I shall have no rest till I am possessed of an appearance equally magnificent. How can I bear to see myself the dingy object I am at present, mingling undistinguished with our race?"

"Proud and heedless idiot," replied the hard old lady, "this same tawdry finery, you so earnestly covet, is but too easily obtained. In order to possess this appearance *it is only necessary to be boiled.*"

MORAL

When the Recruiting Sergeant tempts you with the scarlet uniform, he says nothing about getting you into hot water.

SWAIN. Sc.   C. H. Bennett

The Wolves and the Sick Ass

There were certain hungry carrion-hunting Wolves, who, in a qualm of wonderful charity, paid a visit to a fat old Ass, who lay ill of a bean-surfeit, and was like to die.

"Pray, my good friend," said they, after many protestations of regard, "whereabouts is your greatest pain?"

"Oh, gently! gently!" replied the Ass, as they proceeded to feel his pulse, "for it pricks me just there, where you lay your fingers."

MORAL
The kindness of a legacy-hunter is apt to be killing.

The Ape and Her Two Young Ones

There was a foolish old widowed She-Ape, who had two young Monkeys of twins. She doted upon one of them, whom she countenanced in breaking and pilfering what he pleased; while she only noticed the other to punish him bitterly if he should aggrieve or thwart his brother, but on the whole left him to his own devices.

In the end the spoiled favourite broke out of bounds, and committed a theft away from his mother's cage, and was snapped at by a big Watch-Dog, whose kennel was in a neighbouring Court; while his neglected brother grew up a harmless, active, and amusing Monkey, much respected by all who knew him.

MORAL

A plant may thrive better by the road-side than in a hot-house where a Fool is the Gardener.

THE SPOILT CHILD

The Daw in Borrowed Plumes

A rich vulgar Daw, who had a mind to be genteel, tricked herself out in all the gay feathers which fell from the fashionable Peacocks, and upon the credit of these borrowed ornaments valued herself above all the birds of the air. But this absurd vanity got her the envy of all the high-born birds with whom she wished to associate; who, indeed, upon the discovery of the truth, by common consent fell to pluming her, and when each bird had taken her own feather, this silly Daw had nothing left wherewith to cover her naked vulgarity.

MORAL
Fine feathers do not always make fine birds.

The Lion and the Gnat

As a great majestic Lion was gathering himself up within his lair, to astonish mankind with the wondrous powers of his roar, there came buzzing under his very nose a troublesome Gnat, who challenged him to combat.

"What avail your tremendous lungs and cavernous throat, compared to the melodious pipes of my little organ? and, as for your strength, endurance, and resolution, I defy you to put that point to an issue at once."

The Lion, finding the insect would not be brushed away, was fain to accept the challenge; so to it they went. But the Lion had no chance, for the Gnat charged direct into the drum of the Lion's ear, and there twinged him until in very despair he tore himself with his own paws. In the end the Gnat gained the victory over the noble beast, upon which he flew away, but had the misfortune afterwards in his flight to strike into a Cobweb, where he, the conqueror, fell a prey to a large Blue-bottle Spider.

MORAL
Little miseries are the greatest torments.

The Fox and the Crow

A homely old female Crow, having flown out of a shop in the town with a piece of rich cheese in her bill, betook herself to a fine eminence in the country, in order to enjoy it; which a cunning Fox observing, came and sat at her feet, and began to compliment the Crow upon the subject of her beauty.

"I protest," said he, "I never observed it before, but your feathers are of a more delicate white than any I ever saw in my life! Ah, what a fine shape and graceful turn of the body is there! And I make no question but you have a voice to correspond. If it is but as fine as your complexion, I do not know a bird that can pretend to stand in competition with you. Come, let me hear you exercise it by pronouncing a single monosyllable, which will bind me to you, hand and heart, for ever."

The Crow, tickled with this very civil language, nestled and wriggled about, and hardly knew where she was; but thinking the Fox had scarcely done justice to her voice, and wishing to set him right in that matter, she called out "Yes," as loud as possible. But, through this one fatal mistake of opening her mouth, she let fall her rich prize (in the Fox's shrewd estimation all she was worth in the world), which the Fox snapped up directly, and trotted away to amuse himself as he pleased, laughing to himself at the credulity of the Crow, who saw but little of him or her cheese afterwards.

MORAL

Advice to Rich Widows. When you listen to a knave's flattery upon what you are, you may have cause to regret not having kept your mouth shut upon what you had; and if you possess great store of cheese, be sure that no fortune-hunter will marry you for the mere sake of the Pairing.

The Fox That Was Docked

There was a cunning but over-reaching old Fox, who, having fortified himself within certain Banks for the plucking and eating of unsuspecting Geese, was, nevertheless, unearthed, and pursued by the County Hounds. Being caught by a trap in his flight, he was glad to compound for his neck by leaving his magnificent tail behind him. It was so uncouth a sight for a Fox to appear without this distinguishing ornament of his race, that the very thought of it made him weary of his life. But however, for the better countenance of the scandal, he called the Foxes together, when he made a learned discourse upon the trouble, the uselessness, and the indecency of Foxes wearing long, draggling, bushy tails. He had no sooner finished his harangue, than up rose a cunning old Fox, who desired to be informed whether the worthy Fox that had moved against the wearing of tails gave his advice for the advantage of those that possessed such natural appendages, or to palliate the deformity and disgrace of those that had none.

MORAL
When advice is offered, consider the source.

The Dog and the Shadow

There was a vain and greedy young Dog, who, coming near a certain Shallow Stream called Fashionable Society, saw therein the mere shadow and reflection of a tempting prize (the more so, that he conceived it the property of a luckier Dog than himself), in snapping at which he opened his mouth so eagerly and so foolishly as to cause to fall away from him a rare possession of the same kind which was his own, and which was all he could have desired for his heart's content, but which his lips were never allowed to touch more.

MORAL
Many a fool who has sense enough to get a good wife, lacks the wit to know it.

SMLIV. SC.

C. H. Bennett

The Fox and the Grapes

A lonely She-Fox was fascinated by some grapes which hung high in a certain Vineyard, and, in order to obtain which, she for some time fatigued herself in leaps, friskings, and contortions, more or less graceful, until her joints grew stiff and her bones fairly ached again. But at last, finding her agility decrease, and the grapes farther from her reach than ever, "Let who will, take them," said she, "for I am sure they are as sour as vinegar."

MORAL

It is natural that we should affect to despise what we cannot obtain. In the ball-room of life, the unfortunate "Wall-flower," who has wearied herself out with jumping up in the vain hope of catching a partner, will be found, towards the close of the entertainment, expressing herself in the severest terms on the folly and impropriety of Dancing.

The Mole and Her Son

A young conceited Mole one day prevailed upon his mother to take him out of their dwelling-hole to see some of the fine sights so much admired by the people above them. He proceeded to criticise the surrounding beauties.

"What an execrable view this is," said he, pausing in sight of a beautiful landscape, and twirling his scanty whiskers with an air. "You don't mean to tell me that sky is blue! and the idea of purple grass is positively ridiculous. There's a horse, too, with six legs, and a man taller than his own house. And I'm sure we ought to be able to see the flowers growing on those mountains at this distance! Out of all reason, colour, and proportion. Preposterous!"

MORAL

The fool's tongue is like the rattlesnake's alarum, the providential sign by which we may avoid him.

The Cat's Paw

A cunning old Ape who felt his mouth water at the vicinity of certain tempting fruits which he longed to possess, but which he knew to be guarded in a place too warm for his fingers to venture in, asked a foolish young Cat, whom he saw passing, to come to his assistance.

"I pray you," he said, "lend me your paw to reach those pretty nice things that I require. I am a poor old creature that cannot help himself, and will well reward you for your pains."

The silly Cat complied; but in so doing, burnt his claws so terribly that he was unable to catch mice for months to come, while the old Ape got safely off with the plunder.

MORAL

In the trade of chestnut-stealing, it is the Cat comes in for the kicks, while the Monkey enjoys the halfpence.

SWAIN. sc   C.H. Bennett

The Treacherous Cur

A certain Merchant had a Dog called "Clerk," in whom he placed a particular confidence. He fed the creature from his own table, and, in short, took more care of him than of any of his fellows. This kindness, however, was but ill repaid; for, one day, no sooner was the Merchant's back turned, than the rascally hound flew to the safe, tore it open, and helped himself to all the choice bits that his benefactor, with much care, had scraped together for the sustenance of his own children. But, fortunately, his Master returned in time to detect him in the act, and bade him prepare for punishment.

"Master," said the Cur, in excuse, "bethink you, I am one of your family. I am a Dog who has hitherto borne a good name. Punish me not for this first offence; rather turn your displeasure upon those rascals the Wolves, who make a daily practice of plunder."

"No! no!" replied his Master. "I would rather spare forty Wolves, who rob through want or evil-training, than a Dog like you, who is faithless to trust and insensible to kindness."

So the Dog was bound and carried out of the house, and consigned to the mercy of deep water, with a heavy chain attached to him to keep him from finding his way back again.

MORAL

In the country of Traitors the mere Thief is chosen as king, on account of his superior honesty.

SWAIN sc.   C. H. Bennett

The Dog and the Wolf

There was a gaunt, ragged gipsy of a Wolf who fell into company with a sleek jolly Dog belonging to the spaniel tribe, on the King's highway. The Wolf was wonderfully pleased with his companion, and was inquisitive to learn how he had brought himself to that commendable state of body.

"Why," said the Dog, "I keep my Master's house, and I have the best of meat, drink, and lodging for my pains; indeed, if you'll go along with me, and do as I do, you may fare as I fare."

The Wolf readily agreed, and so away they trotted together; but as they approached the house the Wolf caught sight of the Dog's curiously embroidered collar, from which a kind of gold chain hung down over the shoulder. "Brother," said he, "what is this I see?"

"Oh, that's nothing," said the Spaniel; "a mere social Badge to let the world know whose Dog I am."

"Indeed!" said the other. "If those be the conditions, good-bye. Bare bones and independence, rather than cold chicken with a chain and dog-collar."

MORAL
To the independent spirit, gold fetters are as galling as iron ones.

Swain sc   C. H. Bennett

The Dog in the Manger

A churlish, pampered Cur, who had a comfortable place in a gentleman's well-filled Manger, would from thence snap and snarl to frighten off all poor beasts of draught and burden who passed that way—driven by the hardness of the time of year to beg for provender they could not earn by labour in the fields. This Dog wanted for nothing himself, and yet took an ill-natured pleasure in keeping poor famishing creatures from many a meal, which, but for his officious yelping, they might have enjoyed from his Master's bounty.

MORAL
There would be sunshine in many a poor man's house, but for officious, go-between window-shutters.

The Hare and the Tortoise

What a dull, heavy creature," said a bright-eyed, nimble-footed Hare, "is this same plodding Tortoise! He trudges along in the mud, neither looking to the right nor to the left, only caring to nibble such of the dryest grass and the dirtiest roots as come in his way, and making no more progress in a day's march than I can accomplish in two or three careless bounds!"

"And yet," said the Tortoise (in whose hearing the speech had been made for his humiliation), "although I have neither your lightness of foot, nor the compact and powerful symmetry of your haunches, I will undertake you to run for a wager."

"Agreed," said the Hare, contemptuously. So a goal was named, and away they started together. The Tortoise kept jogging along at his usual rate, and was soon left behind and out of sight by the Hare, who, tired of running alone in a given direction, fell to browsing on choice plants, and then went off to a game of play with certain of his sportive companions, finally making up his form for a snug nap among some tempting long autumn grass: "For," said he, "with my great natural gift of swiftness, I can fetch up Old Humdrum Master Tortoise whenever I please."

But he overslept himself, it seems. For when he came to wake, it was already dark, the weather had changed, and the fields were heavy with clay; and though he scudded away as fast as the ground would let him, he was fain to drop at last half dead with cold and fatigue in sight of the winning-post, which the Tortoise had reached comfortably before him—thereby winning the wager.

MORAL
Genius that may outrun the Constable, cannot overtake Time lost. Or, the race is not always to the swift.

GUILDHALL

INVENT

PLAN

SWAIN.SC.

SPECIFICATIONS   PLAN

C. H. Bennett del

The Fox and the Crocodile

There happened to be an argument once between a quiet cynic of a Fox and a conceited vulgar Crocodile upon the point of Blood and Extraction; the Crocodile boasted of his descent and the renown of his Ancestors.

"Our family," said he, "is of the greatest antiquity. We were princes in Egypt before the foundation of the Pyramids."

"Friend," said the Fox, smiling, and pointing with his claw to certain dabs of mud resting between the coarse excrescences of the speaker's hide, "there will need no herald to prove your gentility, for you carry the marks of your origin on your very skin."

MORAL
No disgrace can arise from a humble origin but the folly of denying it.

The Ant and the Grasshopper

As a rich purse-proud Ant was airing himself at the foot of an old tree, beneath the roots of which lay his vast bonded warehouses of Corn, up came a poor starveling Grasshopper to solicit a grain of barley. The selfish Ant told him he should have laboured in Summer if he would not have wanted in Winter.

"But," said the poor Chirper, "I was not idle: I sung out the whole season. I did my best to amuse you and your fellow-husbandmen while you were getting in your harvest."

"If this is the case," returned the Ant with unpardonable callousness, "you may make a merry year of it, and dance in Winter to the tune you sang in Summer."

MORAL

As the world dispenses its payments, it is decreed that the Poet who sings for his breakfast shall whistle for his dinner.

The Wolf in Sheep's Clothing

There is a story of a greedy Wolf who, having deceptively wrapped himself in woollen clothing marked X 25 in sign of his belonging to the peaceful flock, was, for a long while, permitted to prowl about certain homesteads, where, his real nature not being suspected, he caused most unaccountable decreases in the family store of mutton.

But being in the end discovered by the Shepherd (who was named Inspector), he was, by that watchful guardian of the public pastures, ignominiously stripped and flogged, howling, to the wilderness.

"Why whip you the animal?" asked the neighbours. "Was he not faithful?"

"Faithful!" cried the Shepherd, laying on in wrath. "I took him for an honest watch-dog, and lo! I find him in Sheep's clothing, making sheep's eyes at a foolish ewe, whom he would have eaten out of house and home to satisfy his wolfish cravings, had she not given him her Master's lamb for supper."

MORAL

Beware how you invite a man to dinner on the strength of his outside recommendations. His inside capabilities may astonish you.

The Wolf and the Crane

A ragged-haired, sharp-fanged Wolf, having, through overgorging himself with honest men's property, brought on an uneasy sensation about his throat, which threatened to be fatal, applied to a clever Crane of the long-billed species to help him through his trouble, upon condition of a very considerable reward for the practitioner's pains. The Crane, by skilfully removing certain perilous obstructive matters, brought the Wolf's throat out of danger, and then claimed the fulfilment of his client's promise.

"What!" said the knavish brute. "Have I not let you go without even the mark of my gripe round your own throttle? Be thankful that I have not mangled your lean carcase for you, stripped your head of its knowing wig, and your back of its glossy rustling robe. Expect no greater recompense for saving the life of a Wolf."

MORAL
Abstention from harm is a Rascal's magnanimity.